BELOW DECK: A *TITANIC* STORY

Written by Tony Bradman

Illustrated by Kevin Hopgood

Contents

Chapter One

The *Titanic* was the biggest thing Grace had ever seen in her life. She stood by the harbor with her Auntie Nora, the two of them looking up at it.

"Well, this is where we'll have to say good-bye," said Auntie Nora.

They were near the bottom of some stairs that had been placed against the side of the ship. Many people were climbing the stairs to an open door halfway up.

Grace could see tears in Auntie Nora's eyes. This was hard for them. Auntie Nora was Grace's mother's big sister, and she had taken Grace in at the age of five, after Grace's parents had died. She had been a mother to Grace, and they were very close.

Auntie Nora was always worrying about Grace's future. That's why she had decided Grace should go to live in New York City with Uncle Patrick.

"Things are much better over in America than here in old Ireland," Auntie Nora had said. "There are certainly more jobs. A clever girl like you will do just fine there."

Grace had argued, of course. The thought of being sent to a different country, far away from Auntie Nora, was terrifying. But Auntie Nora wouldn't change her mind. She had written to Uncle Patrick, and he'd written back to say it was a "grand idea!" So here they were, a week later, in a place called Queenstown. They had come by train from Dublin so that Grace could board the ship that would take her away forever.

Now Grace's eyes were filling with tears too, and she hugged Auntie Nora tight.

"Good-bye, Auntie," she whispered. "I won't forget you, I promise."

"Nonsense," said Auntie Nora with a sad smile. "You won't give me a thought once you're on that ship, and so you shouldn't. It's a wonder, all right."

"I don't care how amazing it is," said Grace. "I'll be thinking about you."

But Grace had to admit she was a little excited about going on the ship. The *Titanic* had been built in Belfast, in the north of Ireland, and this was its first voyage. The whole world seemed to be talking about its size and speed and how it would never sink, whatever happened.

"Ah, Grace, you're a sweet girl," said Auntie Nora, kissing her. "You're too nice for your own good sometimes. Just take care of yourself."

They parted at last, and Grace went up the stairs with everybody else. She turned at the top and waved to Auntie Nora in the crowd far below.

Then she boarded the enormous ship.

Chapter Two

A man in uniform checked Grace's ticket and told her how to get to her cabin. There were long hallways that all looked the same, a lot of staircases, and people everywhere. The ship had started its voyage in Southampton, England, and then picked up more passengers in France before coming to Queenstown, the final stop before New York.

Auntie Nora had only been able to afford a third-class ticket for Grace. So her cabin—room F57—was at the bottom of the ship, where everything was cramped and there wasn't any fresh air. It took a long time to find it, but Grace opened the door to her cabin at last.

The cabin had six bunks, five already occupied by a family. They seemed kind, but they spoke a different language, so Grace couldn't communicate with them. There was space under Grace's bunk for her suitcase. There wasn't much in it—some clothes, a piece of paper with Uncle Patrick's address on it, and a photograph of Auntie Nora.

Once she had settled in, Grace realized she was hungry and set off to find the third-class dining hall. The ship was even more amazing than she had imagined. There was just so much to see; so many decks and cabins and other rooms, and she soon got lost in the enormous maze of hallways and staircases.

The second-class decks certainly seemed better than the third-class ones. Grace spotted a cabin with an open door and peered through as she went past.

It was bigger than her own, and there were
only two beds in it. They looked much more
comfortable than the narrow metal bunk she
would be sleeping in. Grace continued up the
decks, curious to see more, but as she was about
to go through a door a man in uniform stopped
her. He asked to see her ticket, and said she
wasn't allowed in the first-class areas.

Grace was disappointed. Everyone back home had been talking about how grand the first-class decks were—it had been in all the newspapers—and now she wouldn't be able to see them. But as she turned down the hallway, she noticed a window that would give her a glimpse into the first-class dining hall.

What a sight it was! The people inside were dressed in fine clothes and sitting at tables covered in spotless white linen. The silver knives and forks and the fine glasses gleamed like something from a fairy tale.

Two boys stood next to Grace and looked longingly through the window too. She recognized them from the third-class decks. Eventually one of them snuck in through the door, grabbed as much cake as he could from a cart, and then ran out again. Somebody at a table yelled, "Stop! Thief!" and several stewards came bustling after the boys. But they were long gone.

Chapter Three

"We'll never catch them," said one of the stewards. "I didn't even see their faces."

Some passengers had come out of the dining room—a girl of Grace's age followed by a man and a woman.

The girl pointed an accusing finger at Grace. "She knows those thieves!" she said in an American accent. "They were together!"

Grace stood rooted to the spot, her cheeks burning.

A steward grabbed Grace's arm. She tried to pull free, but his grip was too strong.

"You'd better tell us where we can find your friends," he said, scowling at her.

"I don't have a clue where they are," said Grace. "And they're not my friends."

"You're lying," said the girl. "You were standing right there with them."

Grace turned to her, suddenly feeling uncomfortable in her patched dress and scuffed old shoes. The girl's clothing looked brand new and probably cost a fortune.

"That will do, Catherine," the man said quietly. Grace realized he and the woman must be the girl's parents. He was tall and dark and wore a tailored suit and bow tie. His wife was fair, and her sparkling dress seemed to be something a queen might wear.

"Your father's right," said the girl's mother. "This is none of our business."

"I was only trying to help," said the girl. "I mean, stealing is wrong . . ."

"Maybe they were hungry," said Grace pointedly.

Stealing was wrong, of course, but Grace hated the way this girl, Catherine, had interfered. She expected Catherine to snap something rude back at her now, but she didn't. She looked down instead, and Grace could see she was blushing.

"Come along, Catherine," the girl's father said firmly, and they returned to their table in the dining room. The steward finally let go of Grace's arm.

"Go away," he hissed at her. "And don't let me see you here again!"

He needn't worry, thought Grace. She had already made up her mind to steer clear of the first-class areas from now on.

By the time Grace went to bed that night, the great ship was well on its way across the Atlantic Ocean. Over the next three days, they were lucky with the weather. The sea was so calm it was like a mirror reflecting the bright April sky, and only a few people were seasick.

Grace missed Auntie Nora terribly, but life on board was interesting, and she was excited about the future. There were people from almost every country in Europe in third class, and they all seemed to get along.

On the fourth evening some third-class passengers had a party. Grace went along and danced and sang with everyone else. It was late, and she felt tired, but she was having fun.

Suddenly, there was a sharp bump that threw Grace off balance, followed by a strange scraping noise.

Everyone stopped dancing and looked at each other.

Chapter Four

It was just before midnight. The party-goers headed up through the hallways toward the main deck, and Grace followed them. A lot of other people from the first- and second-class decks were doing the same.

On the main deck, a large crowd was quickly gathering by the rail. The night air was freezing, and the stars glittered in the dark sky above them. The sea was strangely calm, and everybody was looking up at something white and glittering and enormous drifting past the stationary ship. Grace had never seen anything like it.

"It's an iceberg!" one man yelled. "We've hit an iceberg and we're going to sink!"

People in the crowd looked around, worried, and started to mutter to each other. Surely this man was talking nonsense?

Suddenly the bow of the ship lurched downward with a terrible grinding noise.

Moments later, one of the crew cried out that the captain had given the order to lower the lifeboats. They were going to abandon ship!

Grace felt very scared and alone. She thought of Auntie Nora, and tears filled her eyes. She couldn't believe the *Titanic* was sinking— the newspapers had said that the ship was unsinkable! But now lifeboats were splashing down into the sea. As Grace stood motionless in the chaos around her, word spread that there weren't enough lifeboats for everyone on board, and people started to panic.

Soon there was a lot of yelling and screaming and pushing and shoving. But Grace couldn't leave the ship without Uncle Patrick's address, or Auntie Nora's photograph. She had to go back to the cabin for her suitcase before trying to find a place on a lifeboat.

When Grace reached the staircases leading down to the third-class decks, she found they had been closed off. She had to go a different way, but soon she was lost inside the ship's maze of hallways. "Come on, think!" she whispered to herself. "Now where do I go?"

Just then, the floor shook beneath Grace's feet, and the ship groaned and creaked around her.

The lights flickered above her. Tears streamed down Grace's cheeks as she realized she would have to leave her belongings behind and return to the main deck. She was running out of time and she had never felt so alone. But she pulled herself together, wiped her eyes on her sleeve, and strode quickly toward the stairs.

Getting back to the main deck wasn't easy though. All the hallways were at steep angles now, and in some places Grace had to pull herself along the wall, as if she were climbing a mountain. The lights were flickering even more, and everywhere seemed eerily empty. At last, she spotted someone ahead of her—a girl.

As Grace got closer to her, she realized it was Catherine, the girl who had gotten her into trouble. Their eyes met, and Grace knew Catherine recognized her too.

Catherine ran up to Grace and grabbed her arm, sobbing uncontrollably.

"Please, you have to help me!" said Catherine, her voice cracking. "I got separated from my parents and I'm lost. I don't know what to do . . ."

"Let go of me," Grace snapped. She pulled her arm free. "Why should I help you after what you did? You must be joking!" Grace turned away from her.

"I'm sorry!" Catherine was screaming. "Don't leave me!"

Grace stopped with her back to Catherine and closed her eyes. She remembered what Auntie Nora had said. *You're too nice for your own good sometimes.*

That was true, but Grace also knew it would be wrong to leave Catherine here alone. She sighed, and turned back.

All of a sudden the lights went out, plunging them into darkness.

Chapter Five

Catherine screamed. Grace knew she would have to take charge, even though she felt terrified herself. The two girls stumbled in the dark as she dragged Catherine along the hallway. After a while they came to an area where the lights were still flickering. But now the floor started to shake, and the hallway seemed to tip even more sharply . . .

Grace felt like she was in a nightmare as they turned down hallway after hallway, but at last they came to a staircase that Grace recognized. It would take them to the main deck. They climbed upward—only to discover that things had gotten much worse. The *Titanic* was creaking and groaning like a giant beast in agony, and its front part was now completely under water.

Most of the lifeboats had been launched, but there still seemed to be as many passengers on board the *Titanic* as ever. Grace saw quite a few people struggling into life preservers and jumping into the icy sea far below.

"Come on, this way!" Grace said, and she pulled Catherine toward a lifeboat that hadn't been launched yet. Suddenly a voice called out.

"Catherine! Oh, thank goodness we've found you." It was Catherine's mother, pushing through the crowd. She grabbed her daughter and held her tight.

Catherine's father appeared from the crowd. "We must hurry," he said. "They won't be able to launch the lifeboat if they have to wait any longer."

The three of them started moving toward the
ship's rail, Catherine's father roughly pushing
people out of their way. Grace followed, and
found herself at last looking down into a
lifeboat. It was almost full, but there were still
a few free places. A couple of the crew helped
Catherine and her parents into the boat
through a gate in the rail.

Just as Grace was about to climb down into the boat herself, one of the crewmen put his arm out to stop her. "Hold it," he said, looking Grace up and down. "Only first-class passengers are allowed in this lifeboat!"

"Shame on you!" a man yelled behind Grace. Others angrily called out too.

Grace stood shivering in the cold night air, jostled by the crowd, her eyes filling with tears once more. "But she saved me . . ." Catherine said quietly to her father.

Catherine's father stood up, "Let her on," he said to the crewman. "She's with us."

The man nodded and helped Grace down into the lifeboat.

She sat on a bench next to Catherine, who squeezed her hand. "I couldn't let them leave you behind," said Catherine. "I'd still be lost if it hadn't been for you."

Grace looked up at Catherine's parents, who were watching them.

"Thank you," Catherine's mother whispered to her through an exhausted smile.

Just then, the lifeboat was lowered and they splashed down into the sea. The crewmen at the oars rowed them away from the sinking ship. Grace turned around and saw that the *Titanic* was sliding beneath the water in a huge cloud of steam.

Catherine's father leaned over. "Don't worry Grace," he said, with a kind expression on his face. "We'll take care of you."

As the lifeboat bobbed gently on the waves, Grace wondered what would happen next. She was only halfway to America, but at least she felt safe for now, sitting between Catherine and her parents.